EYE ON THE SKY

WHEN BLIZZARDS BLOW

Gareth Stevens
PUBLISHING

BY THERESE SHEA

Please visit our website, www.garethstevens.com. For a free color catalog of all our high-quality books, call toll free 1-800-542-2595 or fax 1-877-542-2596.

Library of Congress Cataloging-in-Publication Data

Shea, Therese.
When blizzards blow/ by Therese Shea.
p. cm. — (Eye on the sky)
Includes index.
ISBN 978-1-4824-2876-6 (pbk.)
ISBN 978-1-4824-2877-3 (6 pack)
ISBN 978-1-4824-2878-0 (library binding)
1. Blizzards — Juvenile literature. I. Shea, Therese. II. Title.
QC926.37 S54 2016
551.55—d23

Published in 2016 by
Gareth Stevens Publishing
111 East 14th Street, Suite 349
New York, NY 10003

Copyright © 2016 Gareth Stevens Publishing

Designer: Laura Bowen
Editor: Kristen Rajczak

Photo credits: Cover, pp. 1, 9 (main), 18 John Normile/Getty Images; cover, pp. 1–32 (series art) Nik Merkulov/Shutterstock.com; p. 5 Franz Aberham/Photographer's Choice/Getty Images; p. 7 ShaunI/E+/Getty Images; p. 8 (left) Mitchell Funk/Photographer's Choice/Getty Images; p. 8 (right) Scott Olson/Getty Images News/Getty Images; p. 9 (inset) weather.gov/Wikimedia Commons; p. 10 Avatar_023/Shutterstock.com; p. 11 (inset) powerofforever/E+/Getty Images; p. 11 (main) Arctic-Images/Iconica/Getty Images; p. 13 Ed Darack/Science Faction/Getty Images; p. 15 (inset) Richard Arthur Norton/Wikimedia Commons; p. 15 (main) Fae/Keene Public Library/Wikimedia Commons; p. 16 Jeff Wurstner/Wikimedia Commons; p. 17 Niagara Frontier Transportation Authority/Wikimedia Commons; p. 19 NASA/Wikimedia Commons; p. 20 J/J Images - J Morrill Photo/Photolibrary/Getty Images; p. 21 Benoit Daoust/Shutterstock.com; p. 23 Kim Steele/Photodisc/Getty Images; p. 25 (inset, bottom) Henn Photography/Cultura/Getty Images; p. 25 (inset, top) Gordon Wiltsie/National Geographic/Getty Images; p. 25 (main) Bill Hatcher/National Geographic/Getty Images; p. 26 (left) Indigo Fish/Shutterstock.com; p. 26 (right) Cultura Travel/Phillip Lee Harvey/Photolibrary/Getty Images; p. 27 ToskanaINC/Shutterstock.com; p. 28 Julia Nichols/E+/Getty Images; p. 29 Anadolu Agency/Getty Images.

Printed in the United States of America

CPSIA compliance information: Batch #CS15GS: For further information contact Gareth Stevens, New York, New York at 1-800-542-2595.

CONTENTS

Words in the glossary appear in **bold** type the first time they are used in the text.

WHITEOUT!

Imagine you're on a bus with your teammates riding home after a basketball game. It was snowing a bit when you left, but now the snow and wind have picked up. The bus's wheels begin slipping on the icy roads. The bus driver goes slower and slower. Everyone is quiet on the bus watching the conditions get worse.

Suddenly, there's a whiteout. You can't see anything ahead of the bus! Only snowflakes reflecting the bus's headlights are visible. Luckily, this happens just as the bus driver pulls into school. Your coach announces that everyone on the bus will be staying at school until the blizzard is over.

SCHOOLCHILDREN'S BLIZZARD

In January 1888, a blizzard surprised the north-central United States. Temperatures dropped quickly, and snow and wind began. People rushed to get home, but about 235 became lost or died in freezing conditions. Many of these were children on their way home from school. The terrible storm is still remembered as the "Schoolchildren's Blizzard."

There are snowstorms, and then there are blizzards. While both are dangerous, blizzards take danger to the next level.

5

BLIZZARD DEFINED

A blizzard isn't just a lot of snow. The US National Weather Service (NWS) states that a blizzard must have ongoing wind or frequent rushes of wind, or gusts, that reach 35 miles (56 km) per hour as well as a good amount of falling or blowing snow that reduces visibility to less than 1/4 mile (0.4 km). It's this wind in combination with snow that makes a blizzard so unsafe.

Blizzards usually happen when a large mass of cold air meets a mass of warm, moist air. That warm, moist air rises to form snow. The meeting of the air masses also causes high winds.

WARNING OR WATCH?

A meteorologist is someone who studies weather, climate, and the atmosphere. It can be hard for meteorologists to guess, or predict, the timing of a blizzard. That's why they use the terms "blizzard warning" or "blizzard watch." A watch means the storm is expected. A warning means the storm is about to happen or is occurring.

WHAT'S A BLIZZARD?

**LARGE AMOUNT OF
FALLING OR BLOWING SNOW
+
ONGOING WIND OR GUSTS AT LEAST
35 MILES (56 KM) PER HOUR
+
VISIBILITY LESS THAN 1/4 MILE (0.4 KM)**

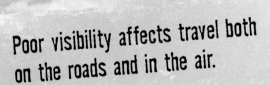

Poor visibility affects travel both on the roads and in the air.

7

Snowfall requires certain conditions in the atmosphere. The air near the surface and in the clouds must be below freezing, but not too cold. Air that's too cold doesn't carry a lot of water vapor, and moisture is needed for snow. It rises into clouds, gathers around bits of dust, and forms ice crystals. When the crystals become heavy, they fall as snowflakes.

It doesn't even need to be snowing to be called a blizzard, though. Sometimes, strong winds can pick up snow that's already fallen. This is called a ground blizzard—and it's just as serious.

WINDCHILL

A blizzard's extremely cold conditions have a lot to do with windchill. Strong winds can make air temperature feel much colder than it actually is. This is called windchill. For instance, a wind that's 50 miles (80 km) per hour combined with a temperature of 30°F (−1°C) can have a windchill temperature of, or "feel like," −12°F (−24°C).

Temperature (°F)

Wind (mph)	40	35	30	25	20	15	10	5	0	-5	-10	-15	-20	-25	-30	-35	-40	-45
5	36	31	25	19	13	7	1	-5	-11	-16	-22	-28	-34	-40	-46	-52	-57	-63
10	34	27	21	15	9	3	-4	-10	-16	-22	-28	-35	-41	-47	-53	-59	-66	-72
15	32	25	19	13	6	0	-7	-13	-19	-26	-32	-39	-45	-51	-58	-64	-71	-77
20	30	24	17	11	4	-2	-9	-15	-22	-29	-35	-42	-48	-55	-61	-68	-74	-81
25	29	23	16	9	3	-4	-11	-17	-24	-31	-37	-44	-51	-58	-64	-71	-78	-84
30	28	22	15	8	1	-5	-12	-19	-26	-33	-39	-46	-53	-60	-67	-73	-80	-87
35	28	21	14	7	0	-7	-14	-21	-27	-34	-41	-48	-55	-62	-69	-76	-82	-89
40	27	20	13	6	-1	-8	-15	-22	-29	-36	-43	-50	-57	-64	-71	-78	-84	-91
45	26	19	12	5	-2	-9	-16	-23	-30	-37	-44	-51	-58	-65	-72	-79	-86	-93
50	26	19	12	4	-3	-10	-17	-24	-31	-38	-45	-52	-60	-67	-74	-81	-88	-95
55	25	18	11	4	-3	-11	-18	-25	-32	-39	-46	-54	-61	-68	-75	-82	-89	-97
60	25	17	10	3	-4	-11	-19	-26	-33	-40	-48	-55	-62	-69	-76	-84	-91	-98

Frostbite Times: 30 minutes · 10 minutes · 5 minutes

Children and older people are particularly affected by windchill.

THE BLIZZARD EXPERIENCE

What's it like to be in a blizzard? People are advised to stay indoors until the storm is over because the wind outdoors is stinging cold. The snow is whipped around, blinding people and **disorienting** them so they can easily lose their way even if walking just a few feet.

Low windchill temperatures mean trouble and possibly frostbite and hypothermia. Frostbite is frozen body **tissue**. Frostbite starts as a "pins and needles" feeling and may result in **blisters** and even dead tissue. However, as long as blood vessels aren't harmed, people can fully recover. Hands, feet, nose, and ears are the first body parts affected by frostbite.

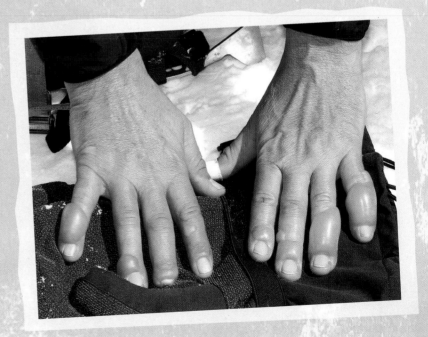

DRESS TO SURVIVE

Being outside too long in the cold and not being dressed for the weather can lead to frostbite or hypothermia, too. Cover every exposed part of the body possible when outside in cold weather: Wear mittens, windproof and waterproof clothes, and a hat and scarf that cover the head and ears.

Extreme frostbite may require affected body parts to be **amputated**.

11

People with frostbite might also suffer from hypothermia. This occurs when the body loses heat faster than it can create it. Normal body temperature is around 98.6°F (37°C). Hypothermia sets in as the body's temperature drops below 95°F (35°C). Hypothermia's first sign is shivering—the body's attempt to warm itself. After that, dizziness, confusion, and tiredness occur. The body's organs may begin to malfunction or even shut down.

The first thing people with frostbite or hypothermia need is to get warm and dry. People with frostbite should get medical attention if feeling and color don't return to affected body parts. **Suspected** hypothermia always requires immediate medical attention.

STAGES OF HYPOTHERMIA

STAGE	SYMPTOMS	BY DEGREE	BODY TEMPERATURE
STAGE 1	AWAKE AND SHIVERING	MILD	90–95°F (32–35°C)
STAGE 2	DROWSY AND NOT SHIVERING	MODERATE	82–90°F (28–32°C)
STAGE 3	UNCONSCIOUS, NOT SHIVERING	SEVERE	68–82°F (20–28°C)
STAGE 4	NO VITAL SIGNS	PROFOUND	LESS THAN 68°F (20°C)

Body heat is lost even faster in cold water than cold air. Get out of wet clothes as soon as possible in the winter.

HYPOTHERMIA HELP

People with hypothermia need special care. Sudden movements can cause them to have a heart attack. They may need to lie in a warm saltwater bath until their body slowly heats up or have their blood warmed with a special machine. Direct heat on body parts can be very risky for victims of frostbite and hypothermia.

13

VERY BAD BLIZZARDS

The Blizzard of 1888, or the "Great White Hurricane," is sometimes called the worst blizzard in American history. It affected the nation along the East Coast from Maine to Chesapeake Bay. New York City was hit hardest of all. Reports of snowdrifts vary from 30 feet (9 m) to 50 feet (15 m) tall!

Many amazing stories are told of this storm. One man reported falling into a snowdrift and onto the hoof of a frozen horse. Another told of getting his false teeth frozen to a lamppost. And yet another remembered walking past the tips of trees in his snowshoes!

THE KNICKERBOCKER STORM

Another great danger of snowfall is the weight it puts on roofs. The Knickerbocker Storm was a blizzard that hit the South and Mid-Atlantic regions in January 1922. About 2 feet (61 cm) of snow collected on the roof of the Knickerbocker Theatre in Washington, DC. It caved in, killing 98 people and injuring 133 others.

More than 400 people had died by the time the Blizzard of 1888 ended, about 200 of them in New York City alone.

No list of the worst blizzards is complete without an account of the blizzard that hit Buffalo, New York, in 1977. On January 28, the temperature dropped from 26°F (−3°C) to 0°F (−18°C) in a matter of hours. Snow began, and the wind rose to 45 miles (72 km) per hour, with gusts of 75 miles (121 km) per hour, creating killer windchill and zero visibility.

The storm came on so quickly that many people were caught at work or outside their home, some in their car. By the time the blizzard ended days later, 29 people had died.

Only 12 inches (30 cm) of snow fell in Buffalo, New York, during the Blizzard of '77. However, the blizzard winds whipped around snow that had fallen days before. This house is almost completely buried!

NATIONAL DISASTER

The areas affected by the Blizzard of '77 were declared federal **disaster** areas. That means the federal government sent in hundreds of soldiers and many pieces of snow-removal equipment to rescue people and clear snow. This was the first time this happened following a blizzard. In all, the blizzard cleanup cost about $20 million.

17

In early February 2010, a blizzard hit the United States that many, including President Barack Obama, called "Snowmageddon," a play on the word "**Armageddon**." The winter storm moved from the West Coast to the East Coast, finally bringing a blizzard that forced life in the Mid-Atlantic states to a standstill.

In all, almost 60 percent of the nation received snow, some parts as much as 38 inches (97 cm). More than 7,000 flights were canceled, and the winds and snow knocked out power for hundreds of thousands of people from Virginia to Pennsylvania. Sadly, 41 deaths were blamed on the blizzard.

THE CHRISTMAS BLIZZARD

The East Coast was again under a blizzard warning on December 26 and 27, 2010. Holiday travelers became stuck in airports when about 5,000 flights were canceled. Winds as strong as 80 miles (129 km) per hour were reported in Massachusetts. This storm is also notable for featuring rare thundersnow, which means lightning and thunder accompanied the snow.

Two more blizzards hit the East Coast in February 2010 after Snowmageddon (pictured here), making it one of the worst winter-weather months in the nation's history. Some called it the "Snowpocalypse."

19

AFTER THE STORM

After any blizzard, there's a lot of snow to remove. This may not be easy. Often, abandoned vehicles block the roads, so snowplows can't clear them. Some places that don't usually get a lot of snow, such as in the South, don't even have snowplows. Sometimes, they just wait a few days for the snow to melt.

Affected cities have to come up with a plan for where to dump the huge amount of snow. Putting it in rivers and lakes can add pollutants to waterways. Special machines can melt the snow, but often it's just put into empty parking lots to slowly melt and go down drains.

Sometimes blizzards are so bad, even snowplows can't drive in them!

HOW MUCH WATER IS THAT?

An inch (2.5 cm) of snow doesn't contain an inch of water. Different kinds of snow contain different amounts of water. Usually, about 10 inches (25 cm) of snow melt into an inch of water. However, some places have heavier, wetter snow, and some places experience lighter, drier snow.

21

METEOROLOGISTS AT WORK

People can make sure they're ready for storms by reading, watching, and listening to weather reports. But how do meteorologists know a blizzard is coming? They know that weather conditions that once created a blizzard may lead to another blizzard.

Meteorologists use the tools available to them, including thermometers to measure air temperature, barometers to record air pressure, and anemometers to find wind speed. **Satellites** can show meteorologists cloud cover and movement, and **radar** is used to locate snow and rain. All these measurements and readings can be entered into powerful weather computers to create models of possible weather outcomes.

BEST GUESS

Sometimes meteorologists forecast a blizzard—causing schools to cancel classes and businesses to close—but no blizzard arrives. Meteorologists can only give an educated guess using the measurements and tools they have. They can look at computer models and decide if they agree. However, the atmosphere is always changing. That's why forecasts can be wrong.

Meteorologists share information with each other. This cooperation and continually improving equipment mean weather forecasts are coming true more often.

23

CAUGHT IN A BLIZZARD

If you find yourself caught outside when a blizzard strikes, the safest thing you can do is find a dry place to stay out of the storm. Blowing winds can lower your body temperature, putting you quickly at risk for frostbite or hypothermia. Try not to let your clothes get wet, as this can further lower your body temperature.

It's very important to keep **hydrated**, but don't eat snow. Instead, collect it in a container and find a way to melt it first, such as near your body. Don't hold it right next to your skin, though, because it can lower your body temperature, too.

SNOW CAVE

Some people who are caught outdoors during blizzards build snow caves to keep out of the high winds and bitter cold. Luckily, snow is a good **insulator**. The snow must be good to pack, however. If it's not good enough to make a snowball, then the snow cave either will be impossible to build or will cave in.

24

People who hike in snowy places, such as on mountaintops, should have knowledge of how to survive in a blizzard.

Many people get caught in their car trying to get home to their family during blizzards. If this is you, stay in the car. It will offer protection from the wind. Tell the driver to keep the car off to save fuel, but turn it on for short periods for warmth. Try clapping or stamping your feet to warm your body.

Tailpipes can get buried in the snow and allow a poisonous gas called carbon monoxide into the car. Crack the windows every once in a while to let dangerous gases out. Also, keep a shovel in the trunk of the car for **emergencies** in case the car gets stuck.

WAIT FOR RESCUE

Another reason it's better to stay in the car during a blizzard is that rescuers will have a greater chance of finding you. You can help them by hanging a piece of cloth out of a car window. This is a sign of trouble. Sadly, people who wander from their car can get lost in blizzard snows.

Driving conditions are dangerous during blizzards. If drivers must get somewhere, they should go very slowly.

27

BE PREPARED

Even if you're at home during a blizzard, there are dangers to prepare for. Blizzard winds can blow down trees, weigh down power lines, and cause your home to lose electricity and heat. Fires in fireplaces and certain kinds of heaters can be dangerous without proper airflow in the house, so be sure to be careful when using these.

Preparing ahead of time with emergency kits and talking with your family about what you'd do in a blizzard situation could save lives. Make sure you have a plan of action for the next blizzard in your area.

If the power goes out, a battery-operated radio can help you know what's going on outside during a blizzard or other storm.

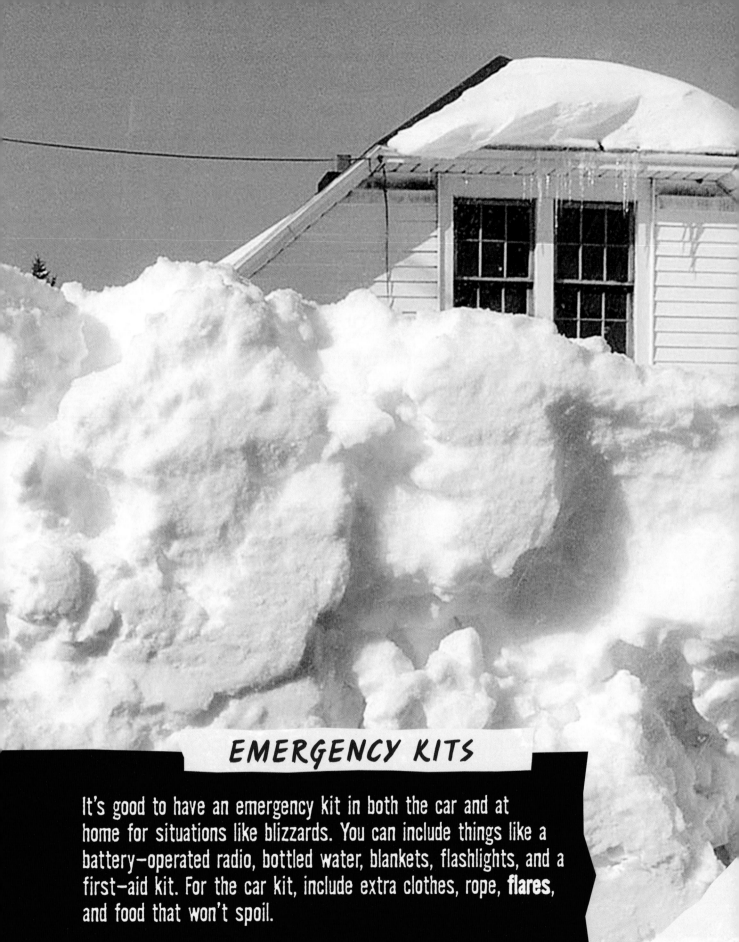

EMERGENCY KITS

It's good to have an emergency kit in both the car and at home for situations like blizzards. You can include things like a battery-operated radio, bottled water, blankets, flashlights, and a first-aid kit. For the car kit, include extra clothes, rope, **flares**, and food that won't spoil.

29

GLOSSARY

amputate: to cut off a body part

Armageddon: a final destructive battle or conflict

blister: a raised area on the skin that contains clear liquid and is caused by injury

disaster: an event that causes much suffering or loss

disorient: to make someone lost or confused

emergency: an unexpected and usually dangerous situation that calls for action

flare: a device that produces very bright light to attract attention

hydrated: having a healthy amount of water in the body

insulator: a material that surrounds something to prevent heat, electricity, or sound from passing through

radar: a machine that uses radio waves to locate and identify objects

satellite: an object that circles Earth in order to collect and send information or aid in communication

suspected: believed likely

tissue: the matter that forms the parts in a plant or animal

FOR MORE INFORMATION

BOOKS

Fleisher, Paul. *Lightning, Hurricanes, and Blizzards: The Science of Storms.* Minneapolis, MN: Lerner Publications, 2011.

Hardyman, Robyn. *Snow and Blizzards.* New York, NY: PowerKids Press, 2010.

Woods, Michael, and Mary B. Woods. *Blizzards.* Minneapolis, MN: Lerner Publications, 2008.

WEBSITES

How Do Blizzards Form?
eo.ucar.edu/kids/dangerwx/blizzard3.htm
Find out more about blizzards, snow, and dangerous precipitation.

The 10 Worst Blizzards in US History
www.livescience.com/31880-countdown-10-worst-blizzards.html
Read about some astonishingly terrible blizzards that have struck the United States.

INDEX